Leo the Vegan Lion

While every precaution has been taken in the preparation of this book, the publisher assumes no responsibility for errors or omissions, or for damages resulting from the use of the information contained herein.

LEO THE VEGAN LION

First edition. March 14, 2023.

ISBN: 979-8215801918

Written by Liom Liom.

A new day in the savannah

A new day begins in the vast savannah of Africa. The sun has just risen and it is slowly getting warmer. The birds are chirping and the first animals are getting ready for the day. Among them are Leo and his family, a group of majestic lions that live in the savannah.

Leo is a young lion and very curious. He has many questions and wants to discover the world around him. Today he wants to go hunting with his father and siblings. They sneak through the tall grass and look for prey.

Suddenly they hear the loud cracking of twigs. Leo and his family froze. They know this is a sign of prey. They move quietly and carefully in the direction of the sound. They are eager to have a delicious breakfast.

As they get closer, they see that it is a herd of gazelles. Leo feels his heart beat faster with excitement. They are so close! But before they can strike, they notice that there is also a group of wildebeest nearby. Leo can see some of the gazelles getting nervous and they all start to interact with each other.

Then something unexpected happens: the leader of the gazelles gives a loud signal and the whole herd flees away in different directions. Leo and his family are left behind, hungry and disappointed. They have no breakfast and have to continue searching for food.

Leo thinks and decides that he has to change something. He no longer wants to just hunt and kill. He also wants to learn how to go without meat. He decides to become vegan and live only on plants.

The other lions laugh at him and say that this is impossible. But Leo is not deterred. He knows he will have to work hard to change his diet, but he is willing to do whatever it takes.

Moral: Leo has realized that hunting and killing animals is not always the best way to survive. He has the courage to make a change and try new ways, even when others tell him it's impossible. This shows that with determination and perseverance, you can accomplish anything you set your mind to.

The lion family on the hunt

Leo wakes up and looks up at the clear sky. He's still hungry, but today he's going to do things differently. He will no longer hunt, but go in search of fruits and vegetables. He tells his brothers and sisters about his plan and they all laugh at him.

"But what about meat?" one of his brothers asks. "That's the best!"

Leo calmly replies, "I know it will be hard, but I want to learn to eat differently. We can also search together and maybe we'll find something good."

His family looks at him skeptically, but Leo remains determined.

They set off and soon pass a small river. A variety of fruits and vegetables grow there. They begin to search and gather.

Meanwhile, they hear the loud roar of lions in the distance. It is another group of lions that is hunting. Leo and his family decide to hide to avoid detection. They watch the other group as they kill one animal after another. Leo realizes that he never wants to live like this again.

Suddenly, the other lions notice them and a fight ensues. Leo and his family fight bravely, but they are outnumbered. Finally, they manage to escape and get to safety.

Leo is disappointed in his peers. He now knows that he has to make his way and that it will not be easy. But he is ready to face this challenge.

Moral: Leo has realized that there are other ways to survive and that killing animals is not always the best way. He has the courage to think and act differently than his peers, even though it is difficult. This shows that it is important to go your own way and not always follow the expectations of others.

Leo meets the elephant

Leo is roaming alone through the savannah. He is looking for new plants and fruits when he meets an elephant. Leo is surprised, because normally lions and elephants don't have much to do with each other.

But this elephant is different. He is friendly and helpful. He shows Leo a variety of plants and fruits that he himself likes to eat. Leo is amazed at all the delicious things he has never tasted before.

The elephant tells Leo about his life on the savannah and how he tries to live peacefully with the other animals. He encourages Leo to do the same and not just focus on hunting meat.

Leo is impressed by the elephant's wisdom and decides to follow him. Together they go in search of more plants and fruits.

Suddenly, they hear a loud roar. It is another lion family that is hunting. Leo is worried and asks the elephant if he can protect him. The elephant nods and together they hide behind a big rock.

The other lion family comes by and looks for prey. But they find nothing and move on. Leo and the elephant are relieved and grateful that they stuck together.

Moral: Leo has learned that it is important to be open to new experiences and not always follow the things you know. The elephant showed him that it is possible to live peacefully with other animals and that you don't always have to eat meat to survive. Together they also learned that sometimes it is necessary to stick together and support each other.

The herd of elephants

Leo and the elephant have decided to go together in search of more plants and fruits. As they continue to move through the savannah, they come across a herd of elephants.

The elephants are friendly and curious and greet Leo and the elephant. They tell the two about their life in the herd and how important it is to work together to survive.

Leo is impressed by the community and the cohesion of the elephants. He realizes that it is not only important to live peacefully with other animals, but also to learn from them and work together.

The elephants invite Leo and the elephant to join them to hunt for food together. Leo and the elephant are thrilled and join the herd.

Together they roam the savanna and find many different plants and fruits. Leo is amazed at the variety and amount of food the elephants can find.

Suddenly, they hear a roar. It is the lion family they have met before. The elephant herd is worried, but they know they are safer in the community.

They decide to stay together and protect each other. Leo and the elephant join in defense and help protect the herd.

In the end, the lion family moves on and Leo and the elephant say goodbye to the elephants. Leo has learned a lot about community and cohesion and is grateful for the elephant's friendship.

Moral: In this chapter, Leo has learned that it is important to work together and form a community to overcome difficult situations. He has also learned that it is important to learn from other animals and that a diverse diet is crucial for survival on the savannah. Finally, he has realized that it is safer in community and that it is possible to work together to overcome challenges.

Leo learns from the elephants

Leo has learned a lot from the elephants. He has learned how important it is to live in a community and work together to survive. He has also learned how to find different plants and fruits and what foods are edible in the savanna.

One day, Leo decides to use his new knowledge and go foraging on his own. He quickly finds some plants and fruits and is proud of himself.

But suddenly he comes across a herd of wildebeest. Leo is scared and doesn't know what to do. However, he remembers the lessons he learned from the elephants.

He decides to stay calm and go near the herd to see what happens. As he does, he observes the wildebeests working together and protecting each other.

Leo realizes that he can learn a lot from the wildebeests. He decides to watch them for a while and learn how they communicate and work together.

While watching the wildebeest, he notices a small wildebeest being attacked by a bird of prey. The other wildebeests immediately gather around the little wildebeest and defend it against the bird of prey.

Leo is impressed by the solidarity and cooperation of the wildebeests. He realizes that in the savanna it is important to work together and protect each other.

At the end of the day, Leo returns to the elephant herd and tells the elephant about his experience with the wildebeests. The elephant is proud of Leo and happy that he has learned so much.

Moral: In this chapter, Leo has learned that it is important to learn from other animals and use their skills to survive on the savanna. He has also realized that it is safer to be in a community and that it is important to protect each other and work together. Finally, he realized that each animal has its role in the savanna and that it is possible to learn and benefit from each other.

The Chimpanzee Gang

One day, Leo comes across a group of chimpanzees playing and frolicking in the trees. They are curious about the lion and come closer to investigate.

Leo is a little worried at first, but then relaxes when he realizes the chimps aren't going to hurt him. They begin to play and interact with each other.

As they play, Leo notices that the chimps are very skilled. They can climb and jump without falling down, and they also have a lot of fun.

8

Leo decides to learn from the chimpanzees and observe them. He realizes that they work together in a gang to fulfill their needs. They help each other climb and find food.

Leo realizes that it is important to have a community that works together to survive on the savanna. He thinks about his friends, the elephants and the wildebeests, and realizes that they also work together to meet their needs.

Suddenly, they hear a loud roar in the distance. The chimps get nervous and start to hide. Leo wonders what is going on and follows the chimps to see what is happening.

As they get closer, they see another lion that has invaded their territory and is stealing their food. The chimps are worried and don't know what to do.

Leo realizes he must help and decides to work with the chimps to drive the other lion away. Together they attack the intruder and drive him out of their territory.

Moral: In this chapter, Leo has learned that it is important to have a community and work together to survive on the savanna. He has also realized that everyone has their strengths and that it is important to learn from other animals. Finally, he has realized that it is important to support and protect each other in order to be successful.

A chimpanzee plays a trick on Leo

Leo had just been resting in the sun when he suddenly felt something on his nose. He shook his head and watched as a chimpanzee sat on the branch above him and winked cheekily at him.

Leo was confused. He had never seen a chimpanzee so confident. He had heard that they were smart and sometimes played tricks, but he hadn't expected this.

The chimpanzee jumped onto another branch and shouted, "Hey, Lion! I have a surprise for you!" Leo was curious and followed the chimp through the jungle.

Finally, they came to a clearing where many chimpanzees were playing and frolicking. One of the chimps, a little guy with a mischievous grin, stepped forward and said, "Hello Leo, my name is Koko. We heard you were vegan and we want to help you get even better."

Leo was surprised and also a little embarrassed. He knew that as a lion he was supposed to eat meat, but he had decided to go vegan. He was happy that there were chimpanzees who wanted to help him.

Koko led Leo to a tree where fruit was hanging. "Here you have a vegan meal, Leo. Eat as much as you want," he said.

Leo ate the fruit and noticed that he felt really good. He felt how much energy he had and that he was full of energy.

"Thank you, Koko," Leo said, smiling. "I think I have a lot to learn from you chimps."

Koko grinned. "We're always here to help you, Leo. Just make sure we don't fool you too much."

Leo laughed, knowing that not only had he made new friends, but that he could learn a lot from them. He finally felt that he was not alone in the savannah, but that there were many animals who were close to him and supported him.

Leo learns from the chimpanzees

Leo was still a little upset the next day about the prank the chimpanzee had played on him. But when he took a closer look at the chimpanzee gang, he noticed that they were very intelligent and resourceful. They could use tools and were able to solve difficult problems.

Leo began to learn from the chimpanzees. He observed how they cracked nuts and how they communicated with each other. The chimps noticed that Leo was curious and offered to teach him how to use tools.

Leo was amazed at how much he could learn from the chimps. He realized that it didn't matter who was stronger or faster, but who was smarter and worked better together. Leo decided to continue learning from the chimpanzees and also to help other animals where he could.

Moral: One should always be open to new experiences and learning from others. Even though we may be stronger or faster than others, we can still learn a lot from them if we listen to them and work with them.

Leo meets a herd of gazelles

Leo was looking for new adventures and learned from the chimpanzees how to sharpen his senses and become more aware of his surroundings. One day he came across a herd of gazelles looking for water. Leo saw that they were thirsty and exhausted and decided to help them.

Leo went to them and introduced himself. The gazelles were scared at first, but when they saw that he was going to help them, they relaxed. Leo showed them a nearby spring and helped them reach the water. The gazelles were grateful and asked Leo if he would accompany them on their way.

Leo was happy to accompany them and protect them on their way. They walked through the tall grass and Leo showed them how to protect themselves from possible danger. They finally arrived at their destination and the gazelles thanked Leo for his help and companionship.

Moral: It is important to help others when you can. Even small gestures of kindness can make a big difference in the lives of others. We should always be willing to share our skills and knowledge and help others when they need it.

Leo decides to go vegan

Leo had had many adventures on the savannah and learned a lot from the animals there. One day he met a group of animals who explained to him that they lived vegan and did not eat meat or other animal products. Leo was surprised because, as a lion, he had eaten meat all his life and thought it was the only way to survive.

The animals explained to Leo that there were other ways to get enough nutrients. They showed him different plants that he could eat to supplement his diet. Leo was curious and decided to try it out.

At first, it was difficult for Leo to change his diet. He missed the meat and had trouble getting enough energy. But he soon noticed that he felt better and had more energy as he got used to the new diet.

Leo decided to go vegan permanently, not only to improve his health, but also to do his part to protect the environment and animals. He realized that he played an important role as a predator on the savannah and that he could do his part without eating meat.

Moral: Choosing to go vegan can have a positive impact on the environment and animals. It is important to find alternatives and have a balanced diet to protect our health and that of the world around us. We should strive to eat more consciously and make our choices carefully.

The challenges of vegan living

Leo had decided to go vegan, and he was determined to maintain his new lifestyle. But it was easier said than done. As a Leo, finding food that met his new ethical standards was difficult.

Leo had to learn how to navigate the savanna as a vegan. He discovered a variety of fruits, nuts and seeds that he had never noticed before. But it was difficult to find enough of them to satisfy his hunger.

One day, Leo noticed the chimpanzees opening coconuts to get to the delicious meat and milk. Leo was excited by this discovery and began to try it himself. Soon he got the hang of it and was able to feed himself coconuts.

Leo also learned how important it was to provide his body with the right nutrients. He was aware that he might not be getting enough protein without meat, but he discovered that there was also a good source of protein in plants. He started eating legumes and tofu to make sure he was getting enough protein.

It wasn't always easy to eat a vegan diet, but Leo was determined to maintain his new lifestyle. He learned the importance of listening to his body and giving it what it needed to stay healthy. And he was proud that he had made a decision that not only benefited him, but also the environment and animals.

The lion pride taunts Leo

Leo was determined to stay vegan, but it wasn't easy. The other lions in his pride started taunting and mocking him because he no longer hunted like a normal lion. They called him a coward and said he was no longer strong enough to hunt with them.

Leo felt very uncomfortable and unsure. He wondered if going vegan was the right thing to do. Maybe he had actually become weak? But Leo remembered why he had decided to become vegan - to live a better life for himself and for the animals.

One day, as Leo was walking alone on the savanna, he heard a lion's voice behind him. It was Simba, the leader of the lion pride.

"Hey Leo, what are you doing here alone?" asked Simba with a mocking undertone.

Leo hesitated before answering. "I'm going for a walk," he said. "I like spending time alone."

Simba laughed. "You really are a strange lion, Leo. But you know what? We don't need you in our pride anymore. We have enough strong lions who can hunt. You're just a burden to us."

Leo felt his heart grow heavy. He hadn't expected Simba to be so cruel to him. But he didn't let it get him down. "I may be different from you, but that doesn't mean I'm weak," he declared confidently. "I decided to go vegan because I believe it's the right thing to do."

Simba laughed again. "That's ridiculous. You'll starve before you ever find another prey that's vegan."

But Leo wasn't ready to give up. "I'll find a way," he said firmly. "And I know it's the right thing to do because I feel better since I went vegan."

Simba snorted disdainfully and turned around. "You'll regret it, Leo," he said. "We'll never see each other again."

Leo looked after him as he moved away. He was sad that Simba and the other lions didn't accept him, but he knew he was doing the right thing. And he was willing to take on all the challenges of vegan life because he knew it made him a better lion.

Leo decides to convince his friends to adopt a vegan diet

Leo was happy with his decision to go vegan, but he knew it would be difficult to convince his friends. He told them about his reasons and showed them how delicious vegan food could be. But his friends were skeptical and laughed at him.

One day, Leo decided to give his friends a surprise. He invited them to a picnic and prepared everything himself - vegan wraps, fruit skewers and nut bars. His friends were surprised at how delicious the food was, and Leo took the opportunity to talk to them about the benefits of a vegan diet.

But despite his efforts, some of his friends remained skeptical and insisted on eating meat. Leo was disappointed, but he decided to be patient and not judge his friends. He knew that change takes time and that by his example and persistence, he might one day be able to convince his friends.

Moral: It is important to be patient and persistent when trying to convince others of a cause. It is also important not to judge or condemn, but instead to set a good example and show others the benefits.

The bird flock parade

Leo hadn't seen a parade this big in a long time! Colorful birds with glittering feathers flew in formation while others danced and sang on the ground. Leo was fascinated and watched the show from a safe distance.

Suddenly, a young bird stumbled up to Leo and asked if he wanted to dance too. Leo was confused at first, but the bird told him that everyone was invited to join the parade.

Leo wasn't sure if he should, but the bird assured him that it would be fun. So, Leo decided to give it a try.

It was difficult at first, but Leo got carried away with the music and danced among the flock of birds. It was an incredible feeling to be part of this community.

When the parade was over, Leo thanked the young bird and asked him why he had invited him. The bird replied, "Because we're all here to have fun together and support each other. It doesn't matter who you are or what you eat, as long as you are happy and kind to others."

Leo thought about those words as he made his way home. He realized that it doesn't matter if you are vegan or non-vegan, it matters if you are kind and respectful to other living beings.

Leo comes across an injured bird and decides to care for it

Leo was out on the savanna when he came across a small bird. The bird was injured and could no longer fly. Leo knew immediately that he had to help the bird. He decided to bring it to his home so he could nurse it and make it healthy.

When Leo got to his cave, he put the bird in a small box to keep it warm and safe. He looked for food for the bird and fed it gently. Leo spent the whole day caring for the bird and helping it get back on its feet.

At night, Leo couldn't sleep because he was worried about the bird. He woke up several times to check on him and make sure he was okay. But when he woke up the next morning, the bird was gone.

Leo was worried and thought that the bird might have died during the night. But when he came out of his cave, he saw the bird flying in the sky. The bird was healthy again and strong enough to fly back to the wild.

Leo was relieved and happy that he could help the bird. He realized that it was important to take care of others and help them when they were in need. Leo decided to always be ready to help and take care of other animals in the savannah.

Full of joy and pride, Leo went back to his friends to tell them about his adventure with the injured bird and to remind them how important it is to be there for each other.

The bird gets well again

Leo took great care of the injured bird and nursed it lovingly. The bird grew stronger day by day and was finally able to fly again. Leo was overjoyed when he saw the bird fly away and go to freedom.

Leo realized that he had done a good thing by taking care of the bird. He decided to continue to be attentive to the needs of other animals and to do what he could to help them when they needed help.

Leo learned that caring and nurturing other animals is an important part of living together in nature. He was proud that he was able to help save the life of an injured bird and decided to continue helping animals in need in the future.

Moral: It is important to be attentive to the needs of other animals and to help them when they are in need. Sometimes a small act like caring for an injured animal can make a big difference and help maintain the natural balance.

Leo learns from the bird how important it is to help others

Leo was proud that he had nursed the injured bird back to health. He felt good that he had helped another living creature. By now, the bird was so strong that it could fly again. Leo decided to observe the bird before releasing it into the wild. He was impressed with the way the bird flew and the way it led its flock.

As Leo watched the bird, he realized the importance of helping others. The bird had shown him that everyone can do something to help others and make the world a better place. Leo decided that not only would he go vegan, but he would actively work to help others.

When he went back to the savannah, he came across a herd of elephants trying to help a sick elephant. Leo remembered how he had helped the bird and decided to help the elephant. He helped carry the sick elephant and brought it water and food. The elephants were grateful and Leo felt good that he could help once again.

Leo had learned a lot from his adventures on the savannah. He had learned that friends can be made in unexpected ways, that everyone can do something to help others, and that it is important to be respectful of other living things. Leo was proud of what he had accomplished and looked forward to having more adventures on the savanna.

The Hyena Attack

Leo and his friends had a long day of adventures. They had tended to an injured bird and walked around the savanna looking for fresh plants. Now they were all tired and decided to rest by the river.

But their rest was abruptly interrupted when they suddenly heard hyenas calling. The animals were notorious for forming packs and searching for prey at night. Leo and his friends drew closer to protect themselves.

The hyenas came closer and closer and they could hear their loud growls. Leo knew they were in danger and they had to act quickly. He called his friends together and told them that they would have to work as a team to fight off the hyenas.

Together they built a defensive line of branches and stones and kept their torches ready. The hyenas charged in, but Leo and his friends held their ground and yelled as loud as they could to drive the animals away.

The hyenas eventually retreated, but Leo and his friends knew they were still in danger. They decided to stay alert and watch out for each other to make sure everyone was safe.

Leo realized that the only way they could defend themselves was by working together and as a team. They had to always be on guard and stand up for each other to survive in the dangerous savanna.

The next morning, they started early to strengthen their defenses and built an even stronger barricade of branches and stones. They knew the hyenas could return at any time, but they were ready to defend themselves and protect each other.

Leo and his friends defend their territory against the hyenas

Leo and his friends had learned a lot about life in the wild. They had learned the importance of helping each other and working together to overcome challenges. But one day, when they were attacked by a horde of hyenas, they faced one of the biggest challenges they had ever faced.

The hyenas were targeting the animals' territory and seemed determined to conquer it. Leo and his friends had to act quickly to defend their home and families. They formed an alliance and used all their strength to fight off the attackers.

It was a tough battle, but Leo and his friends were not ready to give up. They fought bravely and in a coordinated way and finally managed to drive the hyenas away. The territory was saved, and Leo and his friends were proud that they had defended their families and homes.

In the days after the battle, they talked a lot about the importance of sticking together and standing up for each other. They had learned that together they could overcome any challenge, and that it was okay to ask for help when you needed it.

Leo and his friends knew that life in the wilderness was full of dangers and challenges, but they were ready to overcome them as long as they stuck together and supported each other.

A picnic with the elephants

Leo and his friends, the chimpanzees, had been looking forward to a trip to the forest for a long time. This time they decided to make their way to the elephant plateau. Once there, they were warmly welcomed by a herd of elephants.

The elephants had already prepared a big picnic and asked Leo and his friends to join them. There were juicy fruits and delicious salads. Leo and his friends were delighted and enjoyed the food.

During the picnic, the elephants talked about their life in the forest. They told about the challenges they had to face every day to protect their herd. Leo and his friends listened attentively and learned a lot about nature.

After the picnic was over, the elephants accompanied Leo and his friends on a walk through the forest. While there, they showed them some of their favorite places and explained what plants and animals are native to the forest.

Leo and his friends were impressed by the wisdom and kindness of the elephants. They knew they could learn a lot from them and decided to visit the elephant plateau more often.

At the end of the day, Leo and his friends said goodbye to the elephants. They were grateful for the nice picnic and the knowledge they had gained from them. They returned to their part of the forest happy and full of new knowledge.

Leo teaches the elephants how to have a vegan picnic

It was a sunny day in the jungle and Leo decided to take a trip to the river. He packed some vegan snacks and headed out. On the way, he met a herd of elephants who were also heading to the river.

"Hey, Leo!" the elephant leader called out. "Where are you going?"

"I'm going to have a picnic by the river," Leo replied. "Would you like to come?"

"That sounds fantastic!" said the elephant leader. "But we don't have any snacks with us."

"No problem," said Leo. "I have enough for everyone."

When they arrived at the river, they spread out a blanket and started eating. Leo had vegan wraps, and hummus with him. The elephants were skeptical at first, but when they tried the first bite, they were delighted.

"This is incredibly delicious!" said the elephant leader. "How did you make this?"

Leo explained to them how he prepared his meals without meat or animal products and why it was important to choose a plant-based diet.

The elephants were impressed and decided to change their diet. They were delighted to learn that there were many delicious vegan alternatives and that they could also help protect the environment.

Leo was pleased that he was able to convince his friends of the importance of a vegan diet. They all had a nice picnic by the river and enjoyed each other's company.

The search for water

Leo and his friends were searching for water. It had been very hot and dry for days and the last water hole they had found had almost dried up. They knew they had to act quickly to find water before it was too late.

Leo led the group through the area he knew well, but still they found no water. They were tired and hungry, and their mood was getting worse.

"What are we going to do now?" asked the monkey.

"I don't know," replied Leo, "But we must keep searching. If we give up, we will all die of thirst."

Suddenly they heard a rustling in the distance. They ran in the direction of the sound and found a small river that saved their lives. They drank as much as they could and replenished their supplies.

On their way back to the camp, they noticed that the water of the river was very polluted and there were no plants or animals around. They decided to filter and purify the water before using it.

Leo remembered a method he had learned from the chimpanzees to clean the water. They gathered rocks, sand, and charcoal and built a kind of filter. The water was poured through the filter and was then clear and clean.

"We achieved our goal," Leo proudly told his friends, "Don't give up and never lose hope. We learned that there is always a solution if we look hard enough."

The group continued their journey, and each of them felt a little stronger and braver because of the experience they had had.

Leo and his friends help the other animals find water

Leo and his friends were at the river when they noticed that many animals were suffering from the drought and were looking for water. The elephants had found a waterfall, but it was too far away for some of the animals to get to. Leo and his friends decided to help the other animals.

They split up and started looking for water sources nearby. Leo and some of his friends followed the tracks of gazelles that led to a small stream. However, there was not enough water for all the animals. So, they decided to help the other animals reach the elephants' waterfall.

Leo and his friends built a bridge out of branches and leaves to help the animals cross the stream. The chimpanzees helped the smaller animals climb up the steep rocks. The elephants cleared the way and carried the water in their trunks to the thirsty animals.

Finally, all the animals reached the waterfall and there was a great celebration. Leo and his friends had managed to quench the thirst of the animals and bring them together. It was a sign that everyone can help in difficult times by working together and showing solidarity.

Leo and his friends were proud of themselves and happy that they could help the other animals. They learned that it is important to help others and work together to solve problems.

The mouse trap

Leo and his friends were looking for food when they suddenly discovered a mouse trap. Trapped in the trap was a poor little mouse crying for help.

Leo and his friends decided to rescue the mouse. They opened the trap and freed the mouse. The mouse was very grateful and asked Leo and his friends to help it find food, since it had been very difficult to find food lately.

Leo and his friends were very sad about the mouse's situation and decided to help him. They searched for food and brought it to the mouse. They also noticed that many animals in the area were feeling the same way.

Leo and his friends decided to do something about it and started an action to collect food and water for all the animals that needed it. They built feeding stations and water troughs and made sure they were always full.

Thanks to their efforts, all the animals in the area could find enough food and water. Leo and his friends were very happy that they could help the animals and learned that it is important to help others when they are in need.

Leo rescues a mouse from a trap

Leo and his friends were walking through the forest when they heard a loud cry. They followed the sound and found a small mouse caught in a trap. Leo and his friends immediately realized that they had to help the mouse. Leo examined the trap and figured out how to open it to free the mouse.

The mouse was very grateful and asked how he could thank Leo and his friends. Leo said, "You don't have to thank us, we are happy to help." The mouse asked why Leo and his friends were always so nice to other animals, and Leo replied, "Because we all live together in this world and we have to help each other."

The mouse was impressed by Leo's words and asked how she could help. Leo explained that they should always look out for other animals and help them when they are in trouble. The mouse nodded and said that he would.

Leo and his friends continued to wander through the forest, feeling good that they could help the mouse. They knew it was important to help other animals and felt proud that they were able to do so.

Leo learns from the mouse that small animals are important too

Leo was happy when he rescued the mouse from the trap. He felt that he had done something good, but he wondered what the value of that little mouse was in the grand scheme of things.

The mouse sat on his paw and said, "Thank you for saving me, Leo. I'm going to tell you something you may not know. Even small animals like me are important. We help keep the ecosystem in balance. We help pollinate plants, control pests, and more. We may be small, but we have a big job."

Leo was amazed at how much he could learn from the mouse. He had never thought about how important small animals like mice, insects and spiders were to the ecosystem.

From that day on, Leo treated all animals with more respect and understanding, regardless of their size or species. He realized that all animals play an important role in nature and that it was important to protect and respect them.

Leo told his friends about what the mouse had taught him, and they were all impressed by the little mouse's wisdom. Together they decided to treat all animals with more respect and help keep the ecosystem in balance.

The journey to the waterfall

Leo and his friends had an idea: they wanted to travel to the waterfall. It was a long way, but they knew it would be worth it. The waterfall was a beautiful place with clear water and green forests around it.

They started their journey early in the morning and made their way. They had to climb through thick bushes and over big rocks. But Leo and his friends were persistent. They didn't let it get them down and kept going.

When they finally reached the waterfall, they were amazed. It was even more beautiful than they had imagined. They could hear the sound of the water and enjoy the feeling of fresh air and nature.

But suddenly they heard a thud. Startled, they turned around and saw that a big tree had fallen right behind them. They knew immediately that it must have been an earthquake.

Then they saw a herd of animals running toward them. They were hyenas and they looked very angry. Leo and his friends knew they had to defend themselves. They attacked the hyenas and fought bravely.

However, the hyenas were too many and too strong. Leo and his friends fought doggedly, but slowly they began to lose the battle. They were tired and had injuries. But suddenly they heard a loud chirping.

It was a group of birds just flying by. One of the birds saw what was going on and immediately flew to get help. Within minutes, many animals came to help Leo and his friends. Together they fought the hyenas and finally drove them away.

Leo and his friends were happy and relieved. They had learned how important it is to be there for each other and to help each other. The animals at the waterfall were now even closer and knew that they would always stand by each other, no matter what.

The animals take a trip to the waterfall

Leo and his friends decide to take a trip to the waterfall. They pack their backpacks with water, fruits and vegetables and set off. Along the way, they meet many other animals who are also looking for water.

Leo and his friends decide to help them and share their water and food with them. The animals are very grateful and join the group. Together they continue hiking and finally arrive at the waterfall.

Once there, there is great joy. The animals splash in the water and have a great time. Leo and his friends share their food and drinks with everyone and everyone enjoys their time together.

As they rest and relax, they realize that they can accomplish more together than they can each do on their own. They decide to work together more often in the future and help each other achieve their goals.

Leo and his friends realize that cohesion and solidarity are very important and that together they can achieve a lot. They decide to strengthen their friendship and always be there for each other.

Leo shows his friends how to bathe in the waterfall

After Leo and his friends finally reached the waterfall, it was time to take a refreshing bath. But not all the animals were experienced enough to bathe in the waterfall.

Leo explained to his friends how to bathe in the waterfall and how to protect themselves from the strong currents. He also showed them how to climb on the rocks to jump from the waterfall.

The elephants were a little nervous, but Leo and his friends encouraged them to try. After a few tries, the elephants happily jumped into the water and splashed around.

The other animals also had fun swimming in the waterfall and enjoyed cooling off on this hot day.

Leo was proud to have shown his friends how to bathe in the waterfall. It was another proof that he was always willing to help others and share his knowledge and experience with them.

Leo meets a panther

Leo and his friends had spent the day splashing and playing at the waterfall. As the sun slowly set and the animals were about to head back, they suddenly heard a loud growl. They looked in the direction of the sound and spotted a panther leaping towards them.

The animals panicked and tried to flee, but Leo stopped. He knew they couldn't defeat the panther, but he might be able to distract it and buy the other animals time to escape. Leo faced the panther boldly and the panther stopped abruptly.

Leo had stopped the panther and kept it away from his friends. The panther was surprised by Leo's courage and said, "I will let you go, but next time you won't be so lucky." The panther turned and disappeared into the forest.

The animals were grateful for Leo's courage and thanked him profusely. They now knew they could count on each other if they got into trouble. Leo was glad that he could help his friends and that they could all return home safely.

The next day, Leo spent time thinking about the event. He realized that courage and cohesion were important in overcoming difficult situations. And he realized that even the most dangerous animals, like the panther, could have a good heart if given the chance.

The panther challenges Leo to a fight

Leo's heart pounded violently when he saw the panther before him. The big, powerful feline predator had spotted him and was coming at him slowly but determinedly.

Leo knew he was in danger, but he was determined to defend himself. He stood on his hind legs and roared loudly to intimidate the panther.

The panther, however, was not intimidated and attacked Leo. The fight was fierce and dangerous, but Leo fought bravely and skillfully.

Finally, he managed to defeat the panther and drive it away. Leo was proud of himself and happy that he had survived.

But the fight had also shown him how important it was to always be on guard and ready to defend himself. He realized that there were always dangers, but that you could overcome them if you were brave and smart.

Leo returned to his friends and told them about his adventure. They were impressed by his bravery and agreed that it was important to always be alert and ready to defend yourself if you had to.

Leo and his friends now knew that they had to stand together to protect and defend each other. Together they were strong and could handle any adventure that came their way.

Leo shows the panther that you can be strong even without meat

Leo was very surprised when he met the panther. The panther looked at Leo and challenged him to a fight.

"What do you want from me?" asked Leo to the panther.

"I want to challenge you and prove that flesh is the only way to be strong and powerful," replied the panther.

Leo knew he wasn't as strong as the panther, but he also knew he didn't have to eat meat to be strong.

"You may be stronger than me, but I know I can be strong without meat," Leo said confidently.

The panther laughed and attacked Leo. But Leo was quick and skilled and was able to fend off the attack. Leo showed the panther that you can be strong without meat.

"I think I was wrong," said the panther in surprise. "I have never seen such a strong and fast vegetarian."

Leo and the panther eventually became friends, and the panther also learned that you can be strong without meat. Leo was proud to have taught the panther an important lesson and realized that it is not always necessary to harm other animals to be strong.

The big thunderstorm

Leo and his friends had spent a beautiful day in the forest and were on their way back when suddenly a big thunderstorm hit. The sky darkened quickly and lightning flashed in the sky. Leo and his friends began to run quickly to find a safe place, but it was difficult to find a suitable place in the heavy rain and wind.

Finally, they found a cave big enough for all of them. They huddled together and hoped the storm would pass soon. But it was getting worse. The wind was getting stronger and the trees were bending dangerously.

Suddenly they heard a loud bang, followed by a scream. It was one of their friends, hit by a falling branch. They looked around and noticed that they were surrounded by fallen trees and falling branches. They were trapped and could not escape.

Leo knew he had to act quickly. He remembered the skills he had learned from his friends and knew he had to use them to save himself and his friends. He called on his friends to help him, and together they worked to create a way out of the cave.

They dug a tunnel through the soft ground and finally managed to escape from the cave. Outside, the storm had passed and the forest was shrouded in a gloomy mist.

Leo and his friends were exhausted but relieved to be safe. They decided to go home together and warm up. Leo knew that they had only survived because they had worked together as a team. He was proud of his friends and knew that they could accomplish anything if they stuck together.

Leo and his friends have to seek shelter from the thunderstorm

Leo and his friends were on their way home when suddenly a thunderstorm came up. The sky became dark, the wind got stronger and lightning flashed through the sky.

"We have to find shelter quickly," Leo shouted to his friends. "Otherwise, we'll get caught in the thunderstorm!"

The animals ran and looked for a suitable hiding place. Suddenly they heard a loud Crack and crash. A large tree was struck by lightning and toppled right in Front of them.

"That was close," Leo said. "We have to find a safe place to hide before it's too late!"

Finally, they found a cave in a Rock. They crawled inside and waited for the storm to pass. It was loud and scary, but they felt safe.

After a while, the weather calmed down and the animals ventured out again. There were branches and fallen trees everywhere. It was a big mess.

"We'd better go home," Leo suggested. "It looks like the storm did a lot of damage."

The animals nodded and headed back into the forest. Although the storm was very scary, they had protected each other and survived it together.

38

A night under the stars

Leo and his friends had sought shelter from the thunderstorm, but when it had passed, they had lost their way back to their home. It was already late and they decided to spend the night under the stars.

At first, they were a little afraid, but then they began to admire the beauty of the starry sky. The stars shone so brightly and clearly that they felt like they were in another world.

Leo and his friends told each other stories and sang songs until they finally fell asleep. The night was cool and clear, and they slept soundly under the twinkling stars.

The next morning, they woke up and saw that the sun was just rising. It was a magical moment, and they decided to enjoy this special moment and make their way home.

On the way, they thought about how beautiful the night was under the stars and how nature always surprises us. They realized that there were so many things to appreciate and enjoy in life, and to always think positively and make the best of every situation.

When they finally reached their home, they were happy and satisfied that they had spent an unforgettable night under the stars.

Leo tells stories about the stars

Leo and his friends had spent an exciting night under the stars. The next morning, as they all ate breakfast together, one of the animals asked Leo, "Leo, what is the name of that star up there?"

Leo looked up at the sky and smiled. "That's Sirius, the brightest star in the night sky."

The other animals looked up at Leo, impressed. "How do you know that, Leo?" asked the deer.

Leo smiled. "I have heard many stories about the stars. My grandfather told them to me when I was a little lion cub. He told me that every star has a story."

Leo began to tell stories about stars and constellations, and his friends listened attentively. The story of Orion hunting the bull especially impressed the deer. The story of the Great Bear, the guardian of the north, fascinated the owl.

After Leo told his stories, the animals looked up at the sky again, looking for the stars Leo had shown them. The stars were like a canvas on which they could imagine their own stories.

Leo realized that everyone had their own stories and adventures that they had experienced. It was a special moment when the animals sat under the sky and shared their own stories.

Moral: Everyone has a story to tell, and sometimes the stories of others can lead us to share and expand our own stories.

The discovery of the cave

Leo and his friends had set out to explore the area around their jungle. During their journey, they suddenly discovered a cave. They had never seen a cave like this before and were very excited. Leo, who was always brave, suggested that they go inside to see what was inside.

The friends hesitated at first, but finally they agreed and followed Leo into the cave. It was dark and they could hardly see anything, but with the help of Leo's flashlight they found their way. After a few minutes of walking, they reached a chamber in the middle of the cave. The chamber was full of glittering gems sparkling from the walls.

The friends were amazed and fascinated by the beauty of the gems. But Leo was smart enough to know that they couldn't just take the gems. He explained to his friends that these gems were not their property and that they could not just take them. Instead, they should follow the rules and leave the gems where they were.

The friends agreed and left the cave. Once outside, they found they no longer knew the way back. They were lost and it was getting darker. But they knew they had each other and together they would find a solution.

In the end, they found their way back to the jungle. They were exhausted, but also very proud that they had overcome a challenge together. They also realized that sometimes you can find things that don't belong to you, but it is important to respect the rules and respect the property of others.

From that day on, Leo told his friends stories about other adventures they could have together. They were happy and excited about what the future held for them.

42

The animals discover a cave that is perfect for them

Leo and his friends continued to explore the forest and came across a wondrous cave. The cave was large enough to hold all the animals and seemed made for their needs.

There was a clear spring nearby that gave them enough water to drink and bathe in, and it was also cooler than outside, which was nice on hot days.

Leo and his friends decided that this was the perfect place for them. They began to clean out the cave and make themselves comfortable.

Leo helped the other animals set up their areas, and everyone worked together to make the place as comfortable as possible.

Soon the cave was the perfect retreat for all the animals in the forest. They came here to rest, play, and meet their friends. It was a place of peace and friendship where all the animals felt comfortable and safe.

The animals were grateful for the discovery of the cave and for the community they had found here. They knew they had to stick together to survive in the Wild, and the cave was a symbol that together they could accomplish anything.

Leo and his friends were proud that they had found this special place, and they vowed to protect and preserve it so that it would forever remain a safe place for all the animals in the forest.

Leo and his friends collect berries

Leo and his friends were in the cave when suddenly their stomachs growled. They decided to go outside and look for berries. The animals set off and searched the bushes and trees for juicy fruit. It didn't take them long to find a lot of delicious berries.

Leo and his friends began to gather the berries and bring them to their cave. Everyone helped and they were all full of anticipation for the delicious food. But while they were gathering, they noticed something strange. It seemed as if someone or something was watching them.

Leo and his friends stopped and listened. It was quiet, except for the sound of the wind in the trees. But as they continued walking, they suddenly heard a strange growling sound. Leo and his friends froze in fright.

But then they realized that the growl was coming from a small, frightened animal. It was a mouse caught in a trap. The animals rushed to the mouse and tried to free it from the trap. It was difficult, but they finally managed to free the mouse.

The mouse was very grateful and told the animals that it had escaped from the hunters and had accidentally fallen into the trap. Leo and his friends were glad to help and decided that they should all stay together to protect each other.

They returned to their cave and enjoyed their berries. But they knew that they would have to stay on guard in the future to protect themselves and their friends. They had learned that it was important to help each other and stick together, especially in difficult situations.

Leo shows his friends how to make delicious vegan berry jam

Leo and his friends had gathered a lot of berries and decided that they wanted to make jam out of them. But when they talked about it, they realized that no one knew how to make jam.

Leo thought for a moment and then decided to teach his friends how to make vegan berry jam. First, they had to wash and crush the berries. Then they put the juice in a pot and added sugar. Leo explained that they could use agar agar instead of gelatin to thicken the jam.

While they waited for the jam to finish, Leo told his friends why he had chosen to go vegan. He explained that animals deserve just as much respect and love as humans and that there are many healthy, delicious alternatives to animal products.

When the jam was ready, everyone was thrilled! They tried it on toast and it tasted delicious. Leo was proud to have shown his friends that you can make delicious and healthy food without animal products.

A new lion cub

Leo and his friends were playing by the river when suddenly they heard a loud roar. It was the king of the animals, the lion, announcing himself. Leo immediately ran to him and asked what was wrong. The lion answered that he had gotten a new cub and that he wanted Leo and his friends to meet it.

The animals made their way to the lion's den where they met the cute lion cub. It was still small and unsteady on its feet, but all the animals were excited about it. Leo, who was a lion himself, felt especially responsible for the little one and promised to take care of it.

The other animals were very impressed by how gently Leo handled the cub. They realized that even predators like lions can be loving and caring. It was an important moment for all the animals, who now understood that it was not only what animal you were, but also how you behaved that mattered.

A lioness gives birth to a new cub

Leo and his friends were all very excited when they heard that a lioness nearby had given birth to a new cub. They decided to head out to see the cub.

When they arrived at the lioness' house, they saw the newborn lion cub, still very wobbly on its feet. It was so small and cute that they all squealed with delight.

The lioness looked at the animals and said, "Thank you for coming to see my cub. It is my great pleasure to show you, my family."

Leo and his friends were excited about the new family member and decided to help the lioness and her cub where they could. They brought them food and water and stood by them when they needed it.

Leo was proud to be a part of such a loving and caring community of animals. He knew they would all stick together and help each other when it mattered.

Leo and his friends help the lioness raise her cub

Leo and his friends were excited when they learned that a new lioness had given birth to a cub. They decided to help the lioness raise the cub. They gathered food and water and brought it to the lioness and the cub.

The lioness was grateful for the help and allowed the animals to visit the cub and watch it play. Leo and his friends decided to teach the boy a lesson and teach him how to survive in the wild.

They showed him how to gather berries and find water. They taught him how to protect himself from predators and how to communicate with the other animals. The little lion soaked up all this information and grew up quickly.

When he was finally big enough to hunt on his own, he began to break away from his parents and live his own life. But he was grateful for the help Leo and his friends had given him, and he would never forget what he had learned from them.

Leo and his friends were proud of the young lion and happy that they could help him. They knew they had taught him an important lesson - that in the wild it is important to work together and be there for each other.

The return of the hyenas

Leo and his friends had not had a problem with the hyenas for some time. They had believed that the hyenas had left the area and would never return. But they had been wrong.

One day they heard strange sounds coming from a distance. They heard the hoarse laughter and yowling of the hyenas. It was clear that the hyenas had returned.

Leo and his friends were worried. They knew the hyenas were dangerous and could harm them and other animals in the area. So, they decided to gather together and develop a strategy.

Leo explained that they needed to work together to drive the hyenas away. He explained that each of them had a role to play to ensure that the hyenas would not overpower them.

They decided to build a trap to catch the hyenas. Leo and his friends worked hard and made a trap out of twigs and branches. It took them quite a while to finish, but in the end, they had built a pretty solid trap.

They set the trap near the area where the hyenas had been seen and waited for them to fall for it.

That night, they heard the hyenas laughing and yelping again. They knew the hyenas were nearby and looking for prey.

Suddenly they heard a noise and saw that the hyenas had fallen into the trap. They had done it!

Leo and his friends cheered and rejoiced at their success. They had proven that together they were strong and that they would not be intimidated by the hyenas.

They decided to remain vigilant and alert in case the hyenas ever returned. But they also knew that they could work together to solve any problem they would encounter.

Leo and his friends have to drive away the hyenas again

Leo and his friends hadn't had any trouble with the hyenas for a while. But one day they noticed that the hyenas had returned and they were lurking near them.

Leo and his friends knew they had to act quickly to protect their family and their territory. So, they decided to drive the hyenas away.

At first, they tried to drive the hyenas away by roaring loudly, but that had no success. So, they decided to make a plan.

Leo had the idea to use a few of his friends as bait to lure the hyenas away. The other animals would then defend their families and territory in the meantime.

The plan worked perfectly and they successfully drove the hyenas away. The animals were relieved to have their families and territory safe again.

Leo and his friends realized that it was important to work together and develop strategies to protect their community. They were proud that they had accomplished this difficult task and that they had been so successful as a team.

A visit to the hippopotamus

Leo and his friends decided to take a trip to the river to visit the hippo. They had wanted to meet it for a long time and had heard that there was a great watering hole where they could swim and splash.

When they arrived at the river, the hippopotamus was already there and greeted them in a friendly way. It invited them to play with it in the water and showed them some cool tricks how to breathe under water.

During the game, the hippopotamus also told them about its way of life and how important it is to keep the river and its surroundings clean so that all the animals and plants can stay healthy.

Leo and his friends were impressed by the hippo and spent the whole day with him in the water. They had so much fun and learned another important lesson about protecting their environment.

At the end of the day, Leo and his friends said goodbye to the hippo and promised to come back soon. They were grateful for the special day and the valuable lessons they had learned.

Leo meets the friendly hippo

One day, as Leo and his friends were walking along the river, they heard a loud snort. When they turned around, they saw a huge hippopotamus standing in front of them. "Hello friends, how are you?" asked the hippopotamus in a friendly voice.

Leo and his friends were a little scared at first, but when they realized that the hippo was just being friendly, they replied, "We're fine, thank you. How are you?"

The hippo told the animals that this was his regular feeding spot and that he loved to swim in the clear water. Leo and his friends were intrigued and decided to keep the hippo company.

They spent the whole day playing with the hippo and refreshing themselves in the river. The hippo was so friendly and had many interesting stories to tell.

Leo and his friends learned that there are many different personalities in the animal world and that one should treat all animals with respect and kindness.

When it was time to say goodbye, Leo and his friends promised to visit the friendly hippo again soon. They went home happy to have found a new friend.

The hippo tells Leo how important it is to take care of the ecosystem

Leo and his friends were lucky enough to meet the friendly hippo. They were fascinated by its size and calm nature. The hippo invited them to stay by the river for a while and rest.

While they sat by the river, the hippo told Leo and his friends about the importance of taking care of the ecosystem. It explained to them that every part of the ecosystem is interconnected and that if one species disappears, it affects all the others.

Leo and his friends were amazed by this realization and realized how important it is to take care of nature and to respect and protect all species.

The hippo also gave them some advice on how to help protect the environment, such as collecting trash and reducing litter.

Leo and his friends were grateful for the lessons from the hippopotamus and promised to be careful with nature and do everything they can to protect it. They said goodbye to the hippo and set out to share their new knowledge and encourage others to do their part to protect the environment as well.

The desert journeys

Leo and his friends had always dreamed of a trip to the desert. One day, they decided to make that dream a reality. They packed provisions, water, and everything they needed for the trip and set out.

The sun burned hot on their skin and the sand crunched under their feet as they ventured deeper into the desert. But the further they went, the more they realized how inhospitable and dangerous this landscape could be. There was no water, no trees, and no shade. Soon their throats were dry and their supplies were running low.

Leo and his friends began to worry. What if they couldn't find water? How would they survive? They decided to take a break and think over their situation.

At that moment, they heard a noise and saw a man on a camel coming toward them. The man had a big barrel with him and offered them water. Leo and his friends were relieved and thanked him.

The man explained that he was a desert traveler and that he knew how important it was to be well prepared in this landscape. He told them about the dangers of the desert, but also about its beauty and its importance to the environment. He emphasized how important it was to protect the desert and treat it with respect.

Leo and his friends were impressed by the man and his knowledge. They drank the water and continued their journey, but now with a better understanding of the desert and its role in the ecosystem. They decided to do their part to protect the desert and help other travelers in need.

The desert trip was an unforgettable experience for Leo and his friends. Not only did they have the chance to discover a new landscape, but they also learned an important lesson about environmental protection.

Leo and his friends go on a trip to the desert

Leo and his friends had decided to take a trip to the desert. They wanted to experience new adventures and explore nature in a completely different environment.

When they arrived in the desert, they were amazed by the endless expanse and the impressive sand dunes. But they were also worried about the heat and dryness that prevailed in the desert.

But Leo and his friends were well prepared. They had enough water and provisions with them and wore airy clothes to protect themselves from the sun.

During their journey they experienced many adventures. They discovered hidden oases and observed how the desert animals had adapted to the harsh life. They even saw a group of camels resting peacefully in the sun.

But the desert was also dangerous. Leo and his friends had to be careful not to get caught in sandstorms or overexert themselves in the heat.

But despite the challenges and dangers they had to overcome, Leo and his friends were thrilled by the beauty and adventure of the desert. They learned how important it is to be well prepared when traveling and to pay attention to nature and its needs.

When they finally returned to the safari, they were full of new experiences and adventures. Leo and his friends had learned that the world is full of adventure and wonder if you are willing to try new ways and embrace the unknown.

Leo shows his friends how to survive in the desert

Leo and his friends set out into the desert. Although it was very hot, it was also an exciting experience for all of them. Leo knew how to survive in the desert and showed his friends how to find water and protect themselves from the sun.

He explained to them that it is important to always have enough water with you and to always stay in the shade. He also showed them how to dig a cave to protect themselves from the heat. The friends were amazed at how much Leo knew about surviving in the desert.

As they walked along, they saw many different animals that live in the desert. Leo explained to them how each animal has adapted to the conditions of the desert. They also saw some plants that grow in the desert and how important they are to the desert ecosystem.

After spending the whole day in the desert, it was time to go back. On the way back, Leo showed his friends how to build a fire pit and how to prepare food on an open fire. They made a simple dinner and enjoyed the night under the stars.

The next day they returned to the jungle, but they now knew how to survive in the desert and the importance of adapting to the environment. They had had an unforgettable experience and knew they could always count on Leo for survival in the wild.

Farewell to the elephants

It was time for Leo and his friends to say goodbye to the elephants and continue their journey. They were sad to leave their new friends, but they knew they would have many more adventures.

The elephants and the animals of the forest came together to say goodbye to Leo and his friends. They were very grateful for all that Leo and his friends had done for them.

Leo spoke to the animals and said, "I will never forget you, my friends. We made so many wonderful memories together that I will always carry in my heart."

The elephants and the animals of the forest replied, "We will never forget you either, Leo. You and your friends have become an important part of our family."

Leo and his friends bid a fond farewell to all the animals and set off on new adventures. They knew that they would never forget what they had learned from their friends and that they would always have a place in their hearts.

The moral of the story is that friendship and togetherness is independent of the type or size of the animals. When you respect and support each other, even the greatest challenges can be overcome.

The separation from friends

Leo and his friends had reached the end of their journey and it was time to say goodbye to each other. They had shared many adventures together and created unforgettable memories. But now it was time to go their separate ways.

Leo hugged each of his friends in turn and thanked them for the time they had spent together. "I'm going to miss all of you," he said. "But I know we'll see each other again someday."

His friends nodded in agreement and promised to keep in touch. They knew their friendship was strong enough to last across great distances.

As Leo turned to leave, he felt a tear run down his cheek. But he knew he could be proud of all he and his friends had accomplished. And he was sure that they would continue to have adventures in the future - each in his own way.

So Leo and his friends made their way home. Each of them had learned something new and knew that they could always rely on each other. For even though they were now separated, they would remain friends forever.

The Return to the Savannah

Leo and his friends finally returned to Savannah. They were sad that their journey was coming to an end and that they had to say goodbye to their friends, but they were also happy to be back home.

When they arrived at Savannah, they were warmly greeted by their families and friends. They told them about all the adventures they had had during their trip and proudly showed them the treasures they had collected.

But Leo and his friends had also learned something important during their trip: that it is important to protect and respect nature. They had seen how fragile and precious the ecosystem was, and that each and every one of us has a responsibility to make sure it is preserved.

They decided to do their part and started keeping the savanna cleaner and making sure they didn't pollute or break anything. They wanted to make sure that future generations would be able to experience and appreciate the wonder and beauty of nature.

And so ends the story of Leo and his friends, who had embarked on an exciting journey to learn more about the world around them and learned an important lesson about protecting and preserving nature along the way.

Leo and his friends celebrate their return to the savanna

Leo and his friends had finally returned to the Savannah. They were happy to see their home again and celebrate the successes of their journey.

Leo told everyone about their adventures and the things they had learned on their journey. He told them about the friendly hippo who had shown them the importance of taking care of the ecosystem, and about the elephants who had shown them how to work together as a team to overcome challenges.

The friends laughed and reminisced about all the fun and exciting moments they had experienced on their trip. But they were also thankful that they were now back home and could enjoy their Savannah.

They decided to throw a party to celebrate their return and successes. Leo and his friends prepared delicious dishes and had a great time together. They knew that they could accomplish so much as a team and that together they were strong.

The moral of this story is that it is important to work together and work as a team to achieve success. Everyone has their own strengths and talents that can help the team succeed. It is also important to protect and respect nature and the ecosystem to create a healthy and sustainable world for all.

Impressum

LIOM LIOM

AUF DER HÖH 13A

35447 REISKIRCHEN

KONTAKT

E-MAIL: sl350sl@gmx.de

Don't miss out!

Visit the website below and you can sign up to receive emails whenever Liom Liom publishes a new book. There's no charge and no obligation.

https://books2read.com/r/B-A-AOUW-DGQGC

BOOKS2READ

Connecting independent readers to independent writers.

Did you love *Leo the Vegan Lion*? Then you should read *Adventure in Dino Land*[1] by Liom Liom!

[2]

Experience exciting adventures in Dino Land together with Pino and his friends! This paperback brings together all the stories in a fantastic collection that will delight children between the ages of 6 and 8. Join Pino and his friends as they discover a mysterious crystal, return to Dino Land, care for a new baby dinosaur, and many more exciting events. But not only exciting adventures await the little readers. Each story also holds a valuable moral that is conveyed in a child-friendly way. Whether it's about friendship, responsibility or cohesion - Pino and his friends

---

1. https://books2read.com/u/ml8PMB

2. https://books2read.com/u/ml8PMB

always stand up for each other and show how important it is to be there for each other. The handy paperback book is perfect for little hands and is ideal for reading aloud or reading by yourself. The child-friendly language and loving stories take young readers on an exciting journey to Dino Land.